KU-863-073

msc .

27 JAN 1994

01 MAR 1994

**ROTHERHAM PUBLIC LIBRARIES**

This book must be returned by the date specified at the time of
issue as the Date Due for Return.
The loan may be extended (personally, by post or telephone) for
a further period, if the book is not required by another reader,
by quoting the above number                    LM1 (C)

# FACTS AT YOUR FINGERTIPS

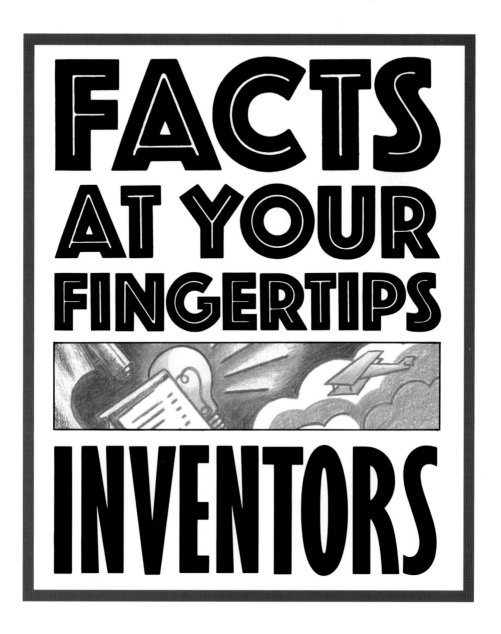

# INVENTORS

## DAVID MARSHALL

SIMON & SCHUSTER
YOUNG BOOKS

Commissioning editor:  Daphne Butler
Design and artwork:  SPL Design
Photographs:  ZEFA
Typesetting and layout:  Quark Xpress

First published in Great Britain in 1992
by Simon & Schuster Young Books

Simon & Schuster Young Books
Campus 400, Maylands Avenue
Hemel Hempstead, Herts HP2 7EZ

© 1992 Simon & Schuster Young Books

All rights reserved

Printed and bound in Belgium
by Proost International Book Production

A catalogue record for this book
is available from the British Library
ISBN 0 7500 1082 7

ROTHERHAM
PUBLIC LIBRARIES

NH 703

J608.7

512330H

SCHOOLS STOCK

# CONTENTS

4

# EARLY

# INVENTIONS

Most early inventions and discoveries were vital to survival. The control of fire—to keep warm. The making of axes and arrowheads—to catch food. The ploughing of the land—to sow crops. ➤

◄ Early people learnt how to make things out of metal. Some were very functional, others highly decorative. Slowly a huge body of knowledge was collected together.

People learnt how to write things down. They learnt how to keep their knowledge so others could read it and learn. Others who would go on to discover new ways and invent better things. ➤

# THE WHEEL

The wheel was probably invented more than once, each time in a different part of the world. Pictures of carts with wheels have been found in Asia Minor dating from 4000-3000 BC. These were a development of the use of tree trunks as rollers. Axles to hold two wheels together came into use soon afterwards. Lighter, spoked wheels first appeared around 2000 BC.

▲ Potters were probably using wheels as simple turntables as early as 3500 BC. About 600-300 BC, both the Greeks and the Egyptians had potters' wheels that spun continuously when kicked.

Wagon wheel ➤

The wheel was the most important invention ever made. In one form or another it is used throughout the world.

▼ Oil press

▲ Spinning wheel

# METAL WORK

▲ The Egyptians buried their kings in splendid style. This beautiful gold mask was placed in Tutankhamun's tomb in 1323 BC.

▲ Molten copper—copper was used from early times because it is easy to melt and work. Today, it is valuable because it conducts electricity and is used in wiring.

Iron is one of the commonest metals on Earth. It is strong, mixes easily with other metals and has many uses. ▼

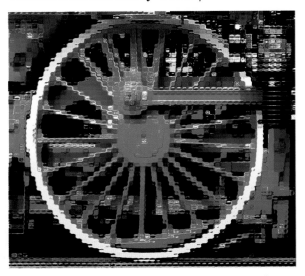

Around 3200 BC, the Egyptians were making jewellery and household items from copper. They also made jewellery and trinkets from gold and silver. Only a hundred or so years later people discovered how to make bronze. Bronze is a mixture of copper and tin and is much harder and tougher than copper for swords, spear tips, armour and storage jars. The Hittites discovered how to produce iron from iron ore in 1500 BC. Iron made good weapons and, at first, the secret was closely guarded, but slowly the knowledge spread throughout the world.

# IRON AND STEEL

Henry ► Bessemer

Iron exists in the ground as an ore containing many impurities. A great amount of heat and energy is needed to extract the pure iron. It was not until 1856, when Henry Bessemer invented the Bessemer converter that large amounts of iron and steel could be made easily and cheaply.

▲ Iron ore is dug from the ground.

◄ Steel is made from the iron ore.

Steel rods stacked ready for sale. ▼

Today, high quality steel is made very quickly by spraying molten iron with a supersonic jet of pure oxygen. The steel is poured out of the furnace into a water-cooled mould. It moves continuously through the mould onto a conveyor belt, where it is rolled and cut to size.

# WRITING AND PRINTING

Picture writing started in the Middle East about 4000 BC, but the first proper alphabets didn't develop until about 1500 BC. The printing of books using blocks of wood was invented in China around AD 868. Chinese characters were carved, back to front, on a single block of wood. About 1045 Pi Sheng invented moveable characters. He made each character out of clay. Once baked, these could be arranged in pages.

▲ Picture writing (hieroglyphics) carved on the Egyptian temple at Abu Simnel about 1300 BC.

Johann Gutenberg ▶

By 1450, a German printer called Johann Gutenberg had made metal letters to use on his printing press in Mainz. Two of his first books were a Bible and a Latin grammar. The knowledge of printing passed quickly across Europe, and started a revolution in the spread of ideas which still continues to the present day.

◀ Each letter was cast on the end of a small metal bar. These fitted in a rack to make a line of type. The lines fitted in a frame to make up the page.

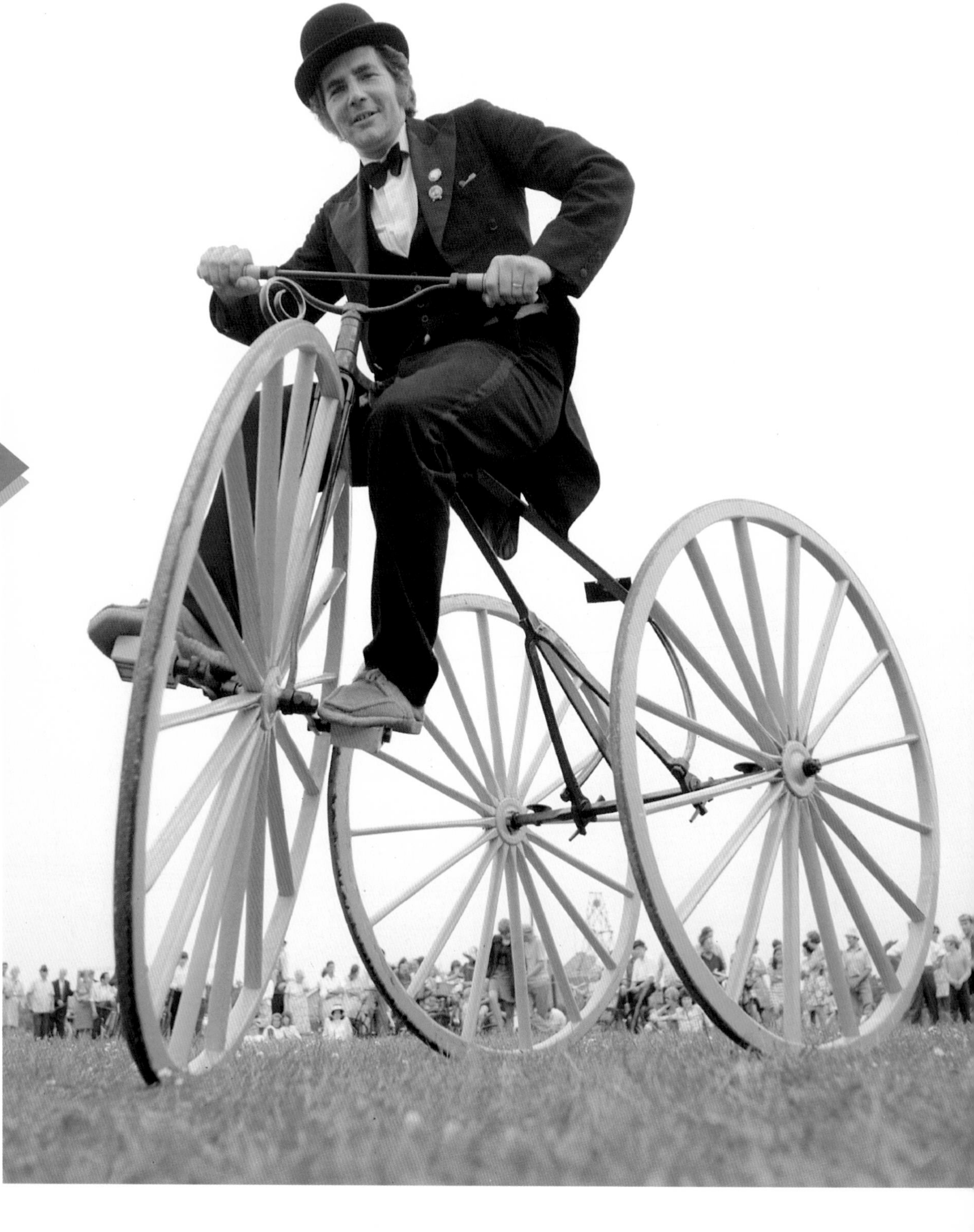

# TRAVEL AND

# TRANSPORT

We live in an age of transport—family cars, high-speed trains and jet aircraft. But these have only become important since about 1950. By 3000 BC the Egyptians were sailing ships on the River Nile. ►

◄ It was the wheel that made the difference, but even then, a few thousand years passed until the 20th century, before the internal combustion engine was perfected and could provide the power.

Flight was always a dream. Legends grew up about men who imitated birds and took to the sky. But again, not till the 20th century did the technology develop enough to make the dream come true. ►

# SHIPS AND NAVIGATION

Wooden boats were sailing on the Nile in Egypt in 3000 BC. It was not until AD 1300, when the Portuguese invented the rudder, that modern ships began to develop. In 1777, the first iron boat was built—it was less than 4 metres long. After 1845, huge iron steamships, fired by coal, were racing across the Atlantic Ocean. Today, engines are fired by diesel oil or nuclear power.

Isambard Kingdom Brunel built ships and railways in the 19th century. ►

Elmer Ambrose ◄ Sperry

▲ All modern iron ships are based on ideas pioneered by Brunel in building *Great Britain* in 1845.

◄ In order to navigate, sailors need to know the direction of north. Compasses have been used on ships since the 11th century. In 1910, Sperry developed a gyroscopic compass which was adopted by navies and merchant ships worldwide. The gyrocompass stays stable relative to the stars, is not affected by the iron hulls of passing ships, and always points to true north and not magnetic north.

# RAILWAYS AND HIGH SPEED TRAINS

In the early 19th century, George Stephenson built steam locomotives to haul coal ore from mine to river mooring. When the first passenger railway opened between Stockton and Darlington in 1825, it was Stephenson's *Locomotion No. 1* that pulled the train. Success led to success, and the Stephensons went on to play a major part in the development of railways worldwide.

The Stephensons, George and his son Robert ►

▲ A copy of Robert Stephenson's famous *Rocket*—the steam engine that won a competition to run on the new Liverpool to Manchester railway in 1829. It reached speeds of 50 kph.

◄ The fastest train today—the French TGV— travels at speeds up to 300 kph. It is quiet, smooth and air-conditioned, and powered from over-head electric cables. Other speedy trains are the Bullet Train in Japan which travels at 250 kph on specially-built track, and Britain's Intercity trains which manage 200 kph.

# THE MOTOR CAR

The development of a motor car was a 19th century dream which changed the everyday life of people in the 20th century. The motor car depended on the building of an efficient petrol engine and the harnessing of its energy to turn the wheels of a carriage. Experimental cars were built mostly in Germany, France, the United States and Britain. Some of the early names like Benz, Ford, Peugeot, Michelin and Rolls Royce are still important names in the industry today.

Motor pioneer Karl Benz ►

▲ A Benz Ideal built in 1901—Benz not only built the first car in 1885, but by 1900 was also the biggest car builder in Europe.

◄ A modern Mercedes being tested for quality before leaving the factory. Gottlieb Daimler built the first Mercedes in 1901, and named it after his friend's baby daughter. The Daimler and Benz companies merged in 1926 to form Mercedes-Benz.

# MASS PRODUCTION

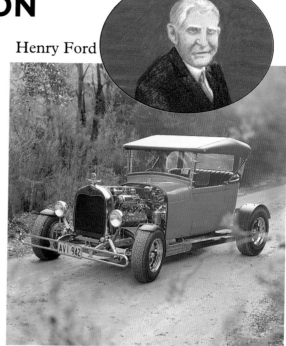

Henry Ford

The first motor cars were luxury vehicles built by hand in small workshops. A small group of skilled workers would work on all parts of the same car. In 1908, Henry Ford built the Model T very cheaply on a production line—cars were passed along on trolleys from worker to worker, each doing only one small job on each car. This way Ford could build 100 cars in one day, and he could sell them at a price ordinary people could afford.

▲ The Ford Motor Company was incredibly successful. Ford believed in supplying a quality product at the lowest possible price and giving his workers a share in the profits.

◄ The assembly line at the Ford Motor Company in Detroit, USA, in the 1960s.

◄ Most modern cars are built by robots on computer-controlled assembly lines. The ideas of mass production are exactly the same as those used by Henry Ford in 1908.

# FLIGHT

The monument to the Wright Brothers at Kitty Hawk, North Carolina. ►

The first flight in an airplane took place on 17 December 1903 at Kitty Hawk in North Carolina, USA. The American brothers Wilbur and Orville Wright flew their *Flyer No 1* for distances up to 230 metres. Today air travel dominates the world.

▲ A copy of the plane in which Louis Blériot became the first person to fly across the English Channel on 25 July 1909. It took 37 minutes to travel 27 kilometres.

In 1976, the supersonic jet aircraft, Concorde went into service across the Atlantic. It carries 100 passengers at speeds of 1600 kph and completes the journey in 3 hours. ▼

▲ Aircraft are serviced with great care between flights— much knowledge and expertise has been gathered since *Flyer No 1* changed the way we travel.

# JET ENGINES

Frank Whittle ►

The first aircraft had piston engines and propellors. The development of jet engines meant that planes could fly faster and higher. The first jet-engine-powered flight was made in a German Heinkel He 178, in 1939, but this never developed as a commercial engine. A gas turbine jet engine was patented in England by Frank Whittle in 1930, but it was not ready for flight until 1941. All British and American jet engines are a development of the Whittle engine.

▲ Jet engines are 80 per cent more efficient than piston engines because no power is lost by moving parts.

◄ Jet engines are checked before each flight, but they can run for 10,000 hours before they need a major service.

# GETTING THE

# MESSAGE

For many years a messenger with a letter was the only way of communicating with people who were far away. Writing is still important but we now also have many other ways of getting our message across. ►

◄ When Marconi showed how messages could be transmitted by radio, the technique had an immediate use for ships at sea. Today, it is hard to imagine the world without non-stop radio entertainment.

When Magellan first sailed round the world, the journey took three years. Today, most parts of the world are just a phone call away—in seconds you can be talking to Hong Kong or Hawaii—unthinkable even a hundred years ago. ►

# RECORDING SOUND

Thomas
Alva
Edison ►

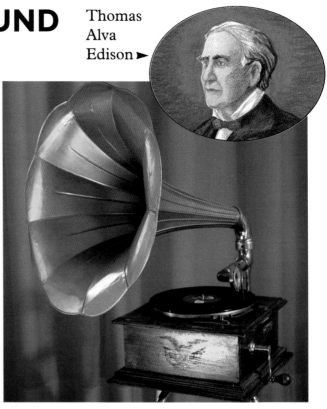

In 1877, Thomas Edison invented a machine to record and playback sound.
He called it a phonograph. The recording was made by a needle scratching a cylinder covered in tin foil. Eleven years later Emile Berliner demonstrated his gramophone using a flat disc instead of the cylinder. By 1892 he had found a way of making copies from a master disc, and the music industry was born.

CK 40518
DIDP 70236

COMPACT
disc
DIGITAL AUDIO

▲ For many years, gramophones did not use mains electricity, but were wound up by a handle. The sound came out of the large horn.

◄ Music today, can be bought on record, disc or tape. Recordings are made in special studios where the sounds are mixed to produce the best effects. The best sound comes from a compact disc. Recordings are made as tiny pits in the plastic surface of the disc and these are turned back into sound by a laser beam in the disc player.

# RADIO AND TELEVISION

Modern radio and television equipment ►

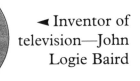

▲ Inventor of radio— Guglielmo Marconi

◄ Inventor of television—John Logie Baird

In 1901, an Italian inventor, Guglielmo Marconi, sent the first message in morse code across the Atlantic by radio. Radio was quickly adopted by shipping lines and navies worldwide, but was not used for entertainment until the 1920s.

In 1925, John Logie Baird, a Scottish inventor, gave the first demonstration of a television picture. In 1936, the world's first live TV service began transmission in London, and the first successful colour television broadcasts were made in America in 1953.

▲ Recording a television programme in a modern studio.

# THE TELEPHONE

Alexander
Graham
Bell ►

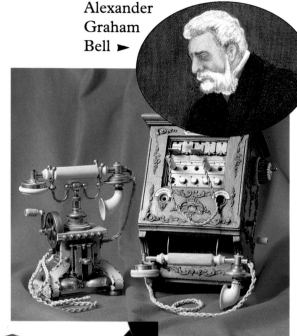

Alexander Bell invented the telephone in America in 1876. The first telephone exchange opened in in 1878, and the first long distance line between Boston and New York in 1884. The first telephone cable was laid across the Atlantic Ocean in 1956, and in 1962, the first satellite link went into service.

Optical fibre telephone cables are made of bundles of very thin fibres of very pure glass. ▼

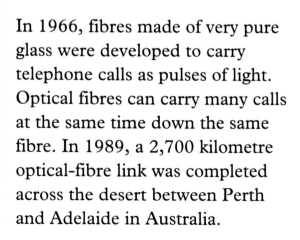

▲ Telephone and switchboard in use in London around 1890.

◄ Push-button telephone in common use today.

In 1966, fibres made of very pure glass were developed to carry telephone calls as pulses of light. Optical fibres can carry many calls at the same time down the same fibre. In 1989, a 2,700 kilometre optical-fibre link was completed across the desert between Perth and Adelaide in Australia.

# COMPUTERS

Charles
Babbage ►

In 1834, Charles Babbage designed but never completed a mechanical calculating machine that could store its results. The first fully electronic computer was built at the University of Pennsylvania, USA, in 1945. It used over 18,000 valves and occupied a whole room. By 1971, the electronics could be fitted onto a single chip of silicon one centimetre square, and computers were much more powerful.

23

▲ Computers used by universities and businesses today are very powerful machines. They can still take up a lot of space, but most of the space is for people, printers, and storage machines.

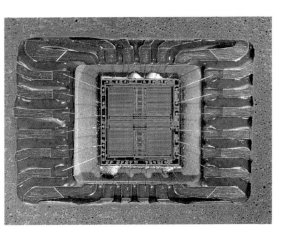

▲ Micro-chip containing the electronics for a whole computer.

During the 1980s the price of personal computers dropped dramatically. In some countries, even very young children have the use of a computer.►

# ELECTRONIC MAIL

In 1979, the British Post Office started a computer information service connecting personal computers to a computer network. It is called Prestel. Subscribers use the service to find information, or to send messages to each other.

Messages are typed into a computer or word-processor and sent by telephone to a central computer. The subscriber to whom a letter is addressed can collect and read it on their own computer, any distance away, by typing in their personal password.

▲ Using a portable computer and a satellite link, computer letters can be sent around the world.

◄ A fax machine is a photocopier connected to a telephone.
You put your letter in the fax machine, and dial the number you wish to send it to. When the fax machine at the other end answers, a copy of your letter is sent down the telephone and printed out at the other end.

# PRINTING NEWSPAPERS

Newspaper reporters can be thousands of miles away from their headquarters. They type in their stories on portable computers and send them in by electronic mail. The stories arrive with the newspaper editor ready to be fitted straight on to the page, again by computer.

On a system invented in Germany in 1965, called Digiset, the pages stored in the computer are projected on to photographic paper. A laser scans the text and transfers it to a printing plate. Other computers control the amount and colour of the ink used for the printing, and the folding and cutting of the final pages.

▲ A printing plate being fitted to the press at the *Financial Times* newspaper in London.

Printers carefully search for mistakes in a proof copy of the *Financial Times* before printing thousands of copies of the final newspaper. ►

# STAYING

# HEALTHY

Until the 19th century, many people died through living in unhygienic conditions, and eating unhealthy foods. Sadly, this is still true for many people in some parts of the world. ►

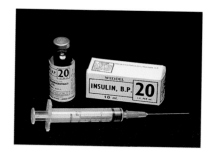

◄ Today we have drugs and medicines to treat most diseases. Doctors have saved millions of lives and relieved suffering by performing delicate operations, but this was not always possible and still isn't for many people.

Operations and medicines are expensive and can have uncomfortable side-effects. But, thanks to many life-saving inventions life expectancy for some people is now well over seventy years of age. ►

# JABS AND POTIONS

In 1796, Edward Jenner protected people from smallpox by infecting them with the much milder cowpox, but didn't understand why it worked. In 1885, Louis Pasteur prepared a vaccine against rabies. He realised that people who had a mild form of an illness then became immune to it. Today, vaccines protect people from unpleasant or deadly diseases. ►

▲ Edward Jenner

Louis Pasteur ▼

◄ Alexander Fleming

◄ Doctors today have a huge range of medicines with which to fight disease.

In 1897, a German chemist, Felix Hoffman, made the first aspirin to relieve his father's rheumatism, and it has been in use as a mild pain-killer ever since. In 1935, Gerhard Domagk discovered Prontosil, the first known sulphonamide—wonder drugs that cure illnesses like meningitis. In 1928, Alexander Fleming had accidentally discovered penicillin, but it was 12 years before Howard Florey and Ernst Chain, found a way to manufacture it. Penicillin was the first of the antibiotics—drugs which kill germs and were to magically change the treatment of disease.

# SURGERY

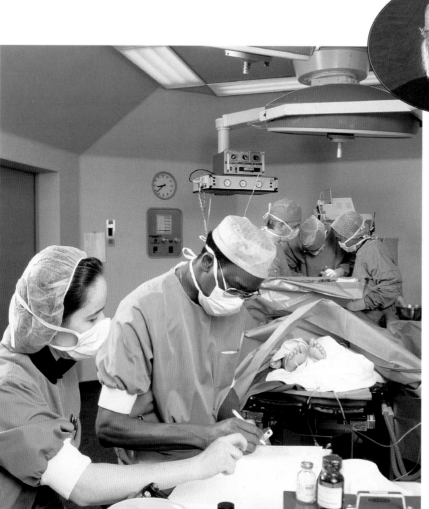

▲ Joseph Lister, Professor of Surgery at Glasgow Royal Infirmary made medical history, in 1865, by using carbolic acid to clean fracture wounds after reading about Louis Pasteur's germ theory.

◄ In modern operating theatres the team work in sterile conditions. An anaesthetist is always there to look after the patient.

The use of anaesthetics and aseptic methods in the late 19th century completely changed the kind of operations surgeons could perform. The discovery of anaesthetics meant that they could carry out operations that would otherwise be too painful, and the use of antiseptics meant that patients stopped dying from infections in open wounds. It was possible to remove blood clots from the brain, operate on ulcers and remove appendices. Since then millions of lives have been saved by an ever-growing list of successful operations.

# FACTS ABOUT INVENTORS

## John Logie Baird
(1888-1946)
Scottish engineer who produced the first successful television pictures. He also worked on producing the first video recorders and discovered the principle of fibre cable optics.

## Sir Henry Bessemer
(1813-1898)
English engineer who invented a successful method of converting iron-o into steel in 1860.
Became a Fellow of the Royal Society and was knighted in 1879.

## Alexander Graham Bell
(1847-1922)
Scottish elocution teacher who moved to North America in 1870 and invented the telephone in 1876 founding the Bell Telephone Company.

## Gottlieb Wilhelm Daimler
(1834-1900)
German engineer who designed the first successful internal combustion engine and formed the Daimler Motor Company which produced the first Mercedes in 1901.
He never met Karl Benz, but the two companies merged in 1926.

## Karl Benz
(1844-1923)
German automobile engineer who produced the first ever petrol-driven car with an internal combustion engine. In 1900, the Benz company was the largest car manufacturer in Europe.

## Thomas Alva Edison
(1847-1931)
American inventor, probably the greatest ever, and a legend in his own lifetime.
A newsboy at 12 years old, he printed his own weekl journal in his spare time to earn money for his chemic laboratory. Just two of his many inventions were the lig bulb and the phonograph (record player).
In 1878, he formed the Edison Electric Light Compar which grew into the mighty General Electric Compan

## Sir Alexander Fleming
(1881-1955)
Scottish bacteriologist who discovered penicillin—the first antibiotic—when a spore flew in through his laboratory window and mould began to grow on one of his experiments.
Knighted in 1944.

## Guglielmo Marconi
(1847-1937)
Italian physicist who invented wireless telegraphy and pioneered radio communication. Founded Marconi's Wireless Telegraph Company.

## Henry Ford
(1863-1947)
American car manufacturer who idolised Edison, pioneered mass production methods and formed the Ford Motor Company.

## Louis Pasteur
(1822-1895)
French chemist who established that germs are the cause of decay and disease.
Invented pasteurisation for the preservation of milk and produced a vaccine for rabies.
Elected to the French Academy for Medicine in 1873.

## Johann Gutenberg
(1397-1468)
German printer who devised a way of casting the letters of the alphabet in metal so they could be used to print books, single-handedly bringing about a revolution in the spread of information firstly across Europe, and then the whole world.
He died penniless, although surviving copies of his books are worth millions.

## George Stephenson
(1781-1848)
English engineer who with his son, **Robert,** built the first successful steam locomotive and became a railway pioneer.

## Sir Frank Whittle
(1907- )
British aviator and engineer who patented a jet engine in 1930 and formed a company called Power Jets to develop it.
Knighted in 1948.

# INDEX